Help Me Understand

What Happens When I Go to the Dentist?

Lisa Idzikowski

PowerKiDS press™

NEW YORK

Published in 2020 by The Rosen Publishing Group, Inc.
29 East 21st Street, New York, NY 10010

First Edition

Editor: Rachel Gintner
Book Design: Rachel Rising

Photo Credits: Cover, p. 7 New Africa/Shutterstock.com; p. 4 leungchopan/Shutterstock.com; pp. 5, 22 michaeljung/Shutterstock.com; p. 9 Henglein and Streets/Cultura/Getty Images; p. 10 Phawat/Shutterstock.com; p. 11 hedgehog94/Shutterstock.com; p. 13 Fusionstudio/Shutterstock.com; p. 14 AboutLife/Shutterstock.com; p. 15 YAKOBCHUK VIACHESLAV/Shutterstock.com; p. 16 science photo/Shutterstock.com; p. 17 puhhha/Shutterstock.com; p. 19 Prostock-studio/Shutterstock.com; p. 20 el lobo/Shutterstock.com; p. 21 santypan/Shutterstock.com.

Cataloging-in-Publication Data

Names: Idzikowski, Lisa.
Title: What happens when I go to the dentist? / Lisa Idzikowski.
Description: New York : PowerKids Press, 2020. | Series: Help me understand | Includes glossary and index.
Identifiers: ISBN 9781725309500 (pbk.) | ISBN 9781725309524 (library bound) | ISBN 9781725309517 (6 pack)
Subjects: LCSH: Dentistry–Juvenile literature. | Dentists–Juvenile literature. | Teeth–Care and hygiene–Juvenile literature.
Classification: LCC RK63.I49 2020 | DDC 617.6–dc23

Manufactured in the United States of America

CPSIA Compliance Information: Batch #CWPK20. For Further Information contact Rosen Publishing, New York, New York at 1-800-237-9932.

Contents

A Dentist

During a checkup, your doctor listens to your heart and your breathing. They look at your eyes and nose. But what kind of doctor checks your teeth? That's right: a dentist. Dentists are doctors who care for a person's **oral** health. They learn how to do this at dental school.

Most dentists treat people of all ages. However, **pediatric** dentists provide care for children, from babies up to teenagers.

Dentists help kids keep their teeth in tip-top shape.

Everyone Sees the Dentist

Moms and dads go to a dentist. Brothers, sisters, grandmas, and grandpas do, too. Even dogs may see a dentist! Everyone needs to see a dentist. It's part of keeping our teeth and mouths healthy.

Chances are, you've been to a dentist before. Do you remember your first time? You might have been a baby. Some doctors say that kids should start visiting the dentist when their first tooth appears. They should at least visit by the time they're one year old.

Dogs need to have their teeth brushed, too!

Let's Go

Imagine that the day has arrived. It's time to see the dentist. You might go with your parents, or you might go with another older family member. How will you get there? Maybe you'll ride in a car or go by bus. Dentists have their offices in many different places.

Inside the office, a person working at the front desk will say hello and ask for your name. They will ask your family member other things about you. After that, it's time to wait your turn.

Pediatric dentist offices often have lots to see and do in their waiting rooms.

$\longrightarrow$

Feelings

Happy, sad, excited—everybody has feelings. Do you ever feel nervous or scared? You might feel this way about meeting someone new, taking a test, or going to the dentist.

Lots of kids feel this way from time to time. It's OK. If these feelings happen when you go to the dentist, talk to the dentist about them. They want you to feel comfortable. They can talk to you about what they're going to do and how they're going to do it.

Many kids bring a favorite toy, such as a stuffed animal, when they visit the dentist.

Time for Teeth to Shine

In time, someone will call your name at the dentist's office. Now what? The first person to check your mouth and teeth may be the **dental hygienist**. She'll clean and floss your teeth. She'll look at your gums. She may take **X-rays** and apply **fluoride** or **sealants**.

The hygienist will probably count your teeth, too. By the time you're seven or eight years old, some of your baby teeth may have already fallen out. When you're about 13 years old, you'll probably have most of your grown-up teeth.

A dentist or dental hygienist uses a large light to see into people's mouths.
→

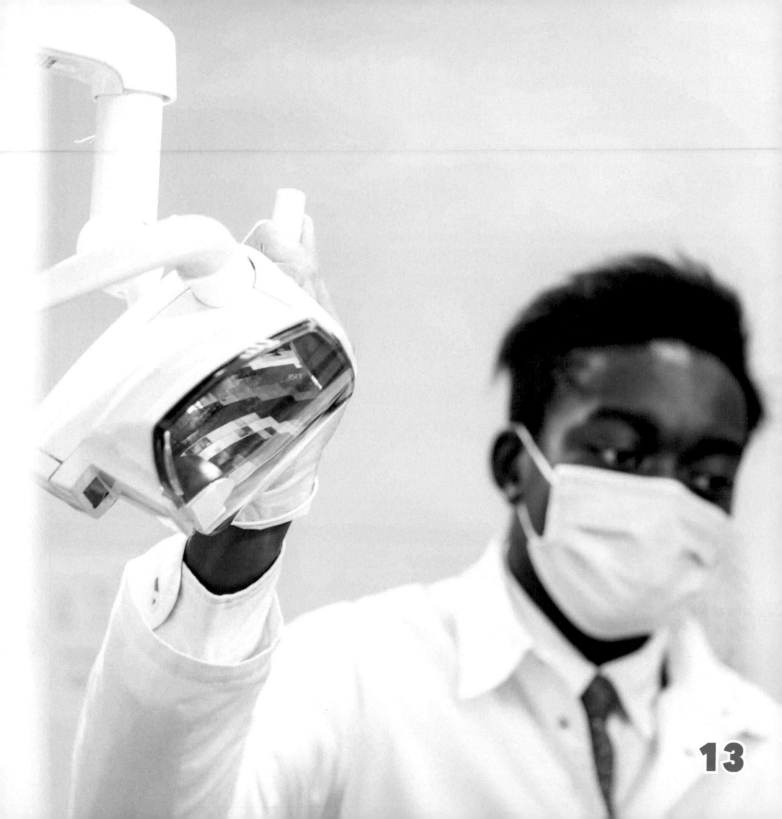

Deep Inside

Imagine seeing through walls to something hidden. People don't have this kind of super vision, though. That's why dentists use X-rays to look deep inside and around your teeth and gums.

To get an X-ray, you'll first have a lead apron, or something similar to a very thick blanket, placed over your chest. Then you'll bite down on a small piece of plastic. Seconds later, it'll be done. X-rays let dentists see tooth problems such as **cavities**.

A visit to the dentist often includes having an X-ray.

Dentist Takes a Look

Now what happens? The dentist will closely **examine** your teeth and mouth. They may ask the hygienist if everything looks OK. If you had X-rays taken, they'll study those pictures.

Then, they'll probably ask you to open wide so that they can look inside and all around your mouth. The dentist will use long-handled tools to help them look around. A small round mirror lets them see your teeth and gums from all sides. They may also use a **probe**.

Dentists use a handy set of tools when examining a person's mouth and teeth.

17

Nice Job!

The dentist will let you know when your dental exam is done. But don't jump out of the chair yet! The dentist may give you a quick lesson on brushing those hard-to-reach back teeth. They may also talk to you about how best to floss.

Most likely, your dentist will ask what you like to eat and drink. They may remind you to drink lots of water and to eat foods that are good for your teeth, including crispy, crunchy fruits and vegetables.

Kids and their parents can enjoy eating and drinking foods that are good for their teeth.
→

Keep Cavities Away

It's important to brush and floss your teeth every day. Dentists say to brush for two whole minutes in the morning and before bedtime. Sealants can also be put on teeth to keep **molars** free from cavities. But even if you do all the right things, you still might get a cavity. The dentist will find it when you visit.

If you get a cavity, you might be scared! But dentists know what to do. They'll take out the bad part and fill the hole in your tooth. They may give you something so it doesn't hurt.

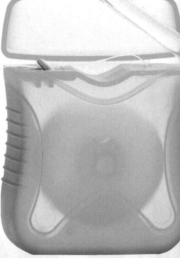

This dentist is using an overhead light to see better.

Until Your Next Visit

Your teeth feel clean, and your smile is shiny and bright. It's time to say goodbye to everyone at the dental office. But don't leave too quickly! Someone in the office will plan your next visit. Dentists suggest a checkup every six months. Don't forget to write the date down.

Your dentist may give you something before you leave—a new toothbrush, toothpaste, and floss. Don't be surprised if there's even a pack of sugar-free gum!

Glossary

cavity: A hole in a tooth made by decay, or the process of being eaten away.

dental hygienist: A person who works with a dentist, often trained to clean teeth.

examine: To look at very carefully.

fluoride: A matter that can prevent tooth decay.

molar: One of several large teeth near the back of the mouth.

oral: Having to do with the mouth.

pediatric: Having to do with children.

probe: A type of tool used by dentists.

sealant: Matter put on teeth to prevent decay.

X-rays: Invisible rays that can be used to take pictures inside the body.

Index

Websites

Due to the changing nature of Internet links, PowerKids Press has developed an online list of websites related to the subject of this book. This site is updated regularly. Please use this link to access the list:
www.powerkidslinks.com/HMU/dentist